Hello DeSign!

Written by
Isabel Thomas

Illustrated by
Aurélie Guillerey

What is design?

You might think a tree is just a tree, but it can also become . . .

a bed!

a boat!

a book!

We can take the tree and use it to make new things. These things didn't grow into their shape, like the tree. They were designed.

To be a designer, you will need your imagination, some paper to draw your ideas . . . and lots of questions!

How will it work?

What will it look like?

What will it be made of?

Who will use it?

Wood is a renewable material. Every time we use a tree we can plant another.

Let's explore the design that is around us every single day.

Good morning! It's breakfast time – and design is all around you from the moment you wake up. Designers start by asking . . .

How will this object work?

This means that most things are designed to do one job really well – a spoon is perfect for scooping up food.

But what can you spot that's **not** doing the job it was designed for?

Are you sitting down to eat your breakfast?

All chairs do the same job – they give us somewhere to sit. But they can work in different ways. Which one would you choose?

Lean back and relax in this chair!

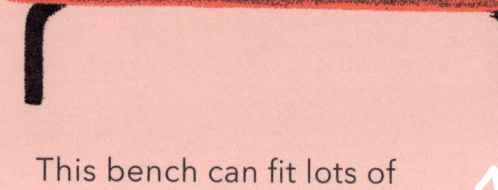

This bench can fit lots of people at once: it's perfect for school assembly.

These chairs are made from just one piece of plastic. Their shape is carefully designed so they can be stacked.

This chair was designed for a messy mealtime.

I'm the happiest chair on this page!

Is this chair for two bottoms? Or is it a chair and table?

Sometimes designers try something completely new – like taking away this chair's legs!

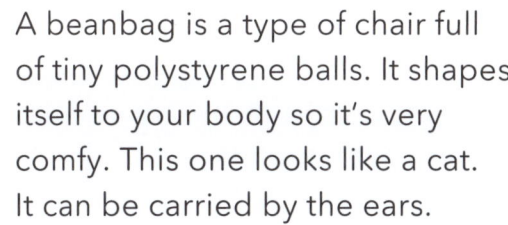

A beanbag is a type of chair full of tiny polystyrene balls. It shapes itself to your body so it's very comfy. This one looks like a cat. It can be carried by the ears.

You'd better not try that with me!

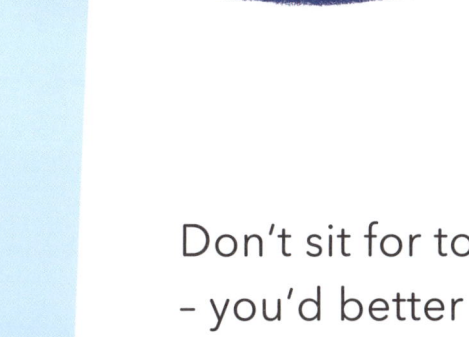

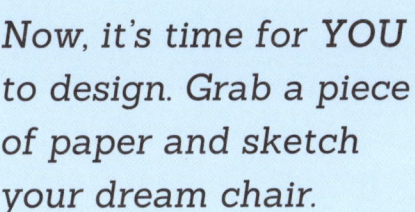

Now, it's time for YOU to design. Grab a piece of paper and sketch your dream chair.

How will it work: will your chair have wheels, or a jetpack so you can fly?

How will it feel: soft like a duvet, or bouncy like a trampoline?

Don't sit for too long – you'd better jump up now because it's time to get dressed.

Designers don't just think about how your clothes look.

They also decide how they work. Your clothes have to work hard!

They keep you warm . . . or cool.

They protect you from the rain
. . . or bounce away sun
(like your sun hat).

I always wear the same coat. It's not designed, it just grows like this. My very own catsuit!

Clothes can show other people who we are, and what we like to do.

Clothes can help us
stand out or blend in.

As well as this, clothes can make us feel brave, confident and happy.

Which of these clothes would make you feel happy today?

We each take more than four million steps every year!

This is why shoes are made of tough materials, like leather, rubber and canvas.

Shoes are designed to work as hard as you.

Kicking a ball

grippy studs

Running and climbing

comfy inside

strong soles

protective shape

Two hundred years ago, the shoes for each foot were exactly the same shape and made of leather. Since then, new materials mean that shoe designs have changed.

The first wellies were designed for fighting! The Duke of Wellington wanted comfortable boots that could be worn on muddy battlefields.

JumPing in puddles

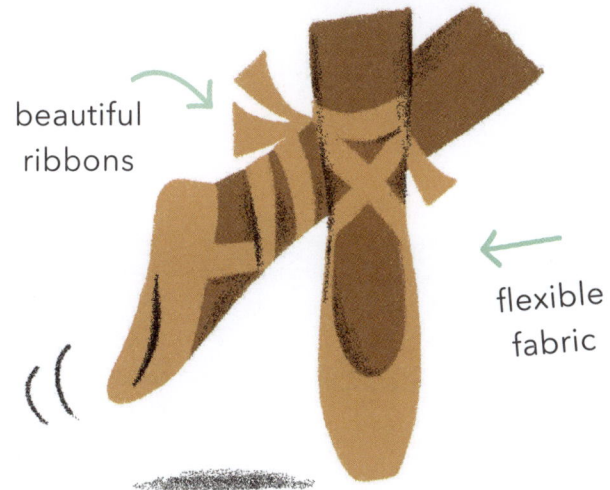

beautiful ribbons

flexible fabric

waterproof

Dancing and twirling

These moon shoes were popular 70 years ago, when space travel began. Children wanted to bounce like astronauts on the Moon!

Design your perfect outfit for today.
What jobs do your clothes and shoes need to do?

Now it's time to go to school!

But what's the best way to travel?
Designers start with these questions . . .

Who is travelling?

Where do they want to go and when?

What do they need to carry?

Is the wheel the best design ever? Before it
was invented 5,200 years ago, people had to
travel everywhere by foot, horse, camel or boat.
Today most vehicles have two, four or more wheels.

14

No design is perfect.
They all have good points and bad points: cars are brilliant at getting us from place to place, but they produce lots of pollution.

Buses and trams have wide doors and low steps to make it easy to get on and off, but lots of stops mean that journeys can take a long time.

Sports cars are speedy and they're designed to look good, but they don't have many seats for your friends!

Microcars are designed for cities. They travel slowly but they help to keep city air clean.

Bikes and scooters are vehicles for just one person. They don't need batteries or fuel – the energy comes from your muscles.

What a great design!

Mountain bikes are designed for adventure. They have wide tyres and a strong frame for bumping over mud and stones.

Electric bikes do have batteries which power an electric motor. This makes pedalling feel easier.

Would you dare to ride a unicycle?

It has no handlebars and usually no brakes!

Scooters with three wheels are easier to balance on. You can steer by leaning from side to side.

It's difficult to take a bike in a car or on a train. That's why some bikes can fold up.

Can you design your dream transport for getting to school?

Will it have wheels? Wings? Space for your friends?

You've made it to school!

Schools are designed to be used by lots of people at once. They have wide corridors, large rooms and lots of toilets.

The furniture is small and made especially for children.

18

Bright colours and bold shapes make the classroom interesting.

Buildings don't just keep us warm and dry. They can change the way people act and feel. This classroom has lots of light. It has places to talk and work together. It has quiet places to sit and be calm.

What differences can you spot between the way your home and your school are designed?

It's time to learn! Grab a pen or pencil and let's get started.

But . . . which one? They work in lots of different ways.

Pencils are filled with soft graphite that rubs off paper. It's easy to rub out mistakes, especially if your pencil is designed with an eraser on the end.

Biros are a type of ballpoint pen invented by a journalist called Laszlo Biro. Some of the first people to use them were Royal Air Force fighter pilots, who needed pens that wouldn't explode in flight!

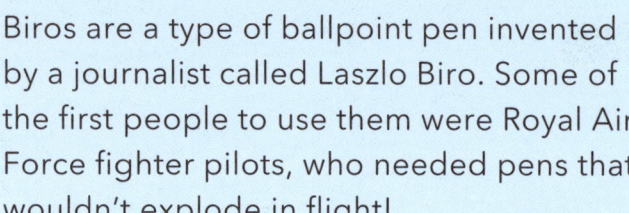

Quill pens were used for 1,200 years! A feather's end was sharpened to make a point, then dipped in a pot of ink.

Ink pens with steel nibs didn't have to be sharpened – but they still had to be dipped in ink all the time.

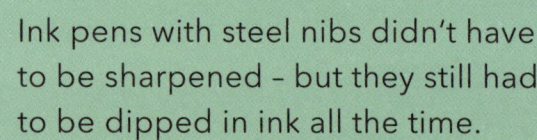

Fountain pens are designed to hold the ink inside, so it flows out like a fountain as you write.

Ballpoint pens are one of the most successful designs ever. The quick-drying ink doesn't smudge, so they can write on a moving plane, underwater and even upside down! This one has retractable inks so you can change colour.

Digital pens don't use ink at all! You can use them on a digital pad and the writing or drawing appears on a screen.

Design the ideal pencil. Will it light up when you make a spelling mistake? Will it sharpen itself? You're the designer, so you can decide.

At last, it's time for lunch.

Have you noticed that most of our food and drink comes in something that has been designed?

Food packaging has two jobs. It keeps food fresh, clean and safe to eat. It also makes the food look nice, so we want to eat it!

Designers don't get everything right first time. It took 10,000 tries to design the first plastic bottle! And this famous invention is still changing. Throw-away plastic bottles pollute the planet, so they are being replaced with bottles that can be refilled again and again.

Lunch trays have lots of compartments to separate different foods.

Designers don't just think about what people need. They think about what the planet needs, too. Metal cutlery can be washed and used over and over again.

Design your perfect lunchbox. What will it be made from? Will it be a material that's easy to wipe clean? Will it be decorated with your favourite things? Or see-through so you always know what's for lunch?

Does the shape and colour of a lunchbox matter? Different designs don't change the taste of the food, but they can make us feel happy.

The bell has rung for breaktime!

Did you know that many popular sports were invented by children in playgrounds? Children are good at finding new ways to play games. Sometimes this leads to the design of brand new sports equipment!

Balls have been used in sports for thousands of years. The first balls were made with animal skins or stomachs - yuck! Their shape hasn't changed, but luckily the materials have.

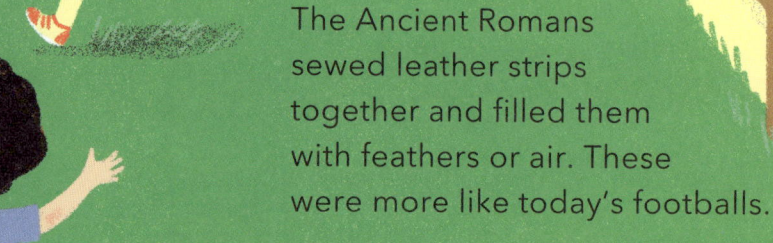

Football is the most popular ball game in the world. The latest balls have microchips hidden inside, so they can 'speak' to smartphones!

The Ancient Romans sewed leather strips together and filled them with feathers or air. These were more like today's footballs.

Frisbees began as tins to cook pies! Children liked to throw them through the air. The first plastic frisbees were made in 1948, and became popular around the world.

You might play with skipping ropes in breaktime. But have you heard of the 'elephant', 'toad' and 'egg beater'? They're all skipping techniques!

Can you design a new playground game? Is it a one-person game, or a new game for everyone to join in?

School's out! And it's time to go home – but, uh-oh, it's raining.

When it starts raining, umbrellas pop up everywhere.

Today, most umbrellas are made in factories. They use light metals like aluminium, and waterproof materials like polyester. There are many different designs to choose from . . .

Designers can make new designs to fix a problem – this umbrella doesn't blow inside out. It's shorter at the front, which means the wind flows smoothly over it. What a clever design!

A hundred years ago, umbrella handles were designed to make each umbrella special. This handle is shaped like a vulture. What kind of person do you think would have used it?

You made it home without getting too wet. Now it's time to play!

We play because it's fun, but it's also the way we learn about the world.

Toys are designed so we can . . .

build and make . . .

imagine stories . . .

follow rules . . . or make up our own!

Is this a table, or a doll's house?
It's a clever design that does two jobs!

A hundred years ago, children used real stone bricks to design their own buildings.

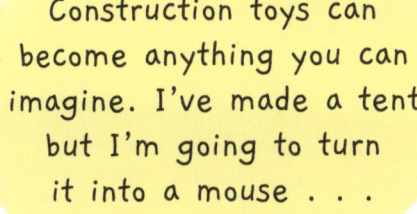

Then wood or rubber bricks that could lock together became popular – because they can be built in so many different ways. The first plastic Lego™ bricks were sold in 1953. Now 75 billion bricks are sold every year! The careful design means that any of the 3,700 different bricks can be joined to each other.

The latest construction kits use small motors and computer chips, so you can build models that move on their own!

Toys used to be handmade by children or their parents at home.

They used materials that were easy to shape with simple tools, such as clay, wood and papier mâché.

Children around the world still design and make their own toys. All of these toys were made using things that would have been thrown away!

This helicopter was made in South Africa using scraps of metal.

Today, many new toys are made in factories. Plastic is the most popular material. It is easy to change its colour and shape, it can be hard or soft, and it doesn't break easily.

But plastic can harm the environment when we throw it away: it stays underground or floats in rivers and seas for hundreds of years. Designers are finding new ways to solve this problem.

This rocket is made from recycled cardboard.

You can help! Instead of asking for new plastic toys, design your own toys using something you would normally throw away. It could be a tin can robot, or a cardboard castle. A wrapping paper kite, or a board game made with bottle tops. Can you turn rubbish into treasure?

Not long until bedtime, so get ready to brush your teeth.

For thousands of years, people cleaned their teeth by rubbing them with rags, or by chomping on twigs! Thanks to designers, cleaning your teeth today is much easier.

Toothbrushes with bristles were invented in China, more than 500 years ago. The bristles were actually thick animal hairs! The handles were made from bamboo or bone.

Today's toothbrushes have plastic bristles. The handles are made from plastic too. It's harder for germs to live and grow on plastic.

We only use toothbrushes for a few months before replacing them. That's a lot of plastic to throw away! To solve this problem, some designs have gone back to using bamboo handles.

Brushing your teeth can feel boring, so designers have changed how toothbrushes look and work. Some toothbrushes have a flashing light, or they beep when you've brushed for long enough. Some toothbrushes are funny shapes, or they're simply your favourite colour.

How would you design a toothbrush to make brushing your teeth fun? Would it play a song?

Now it's nearly bedtime!

Lots of things in this bedroom look like something else. The designers were inspired by nature.

This bookshelf looks like a snake.

This light is designed to look like a vegetable called an artichoke.

This desk and stool look like a pair of toadstools.

This designer was inspired by elephants. Children can sit on the seat – or play with it.

Ideas from nature can help designs work better too. One day, an engineer and his dog went for a walk. The dog came back covered in burrs. These are seeds that are covered in tiny spikes, so they tangle in animal fur. The engineer used this idea to design Velcro™. You probably have Velcro™ on your shoes, and maybe on your coat and school bag as well!

I love getting into my animal pyjamas!

How would you design your dream bedroom?
Would nature inspire you too?

Before you sleep it's time for a story.

Which book did you choose? Why did you choose it?
Was it because of the way it's designed?

The cover of a book gives us information
about what might be inside.

Pick me!

Book designers start with questions . . .

Who will read the book?

Should there be pictures?

Should the words be

large or small?

Pick me!

How many words should
there be on each page?

Pick me!

Even the letters used to write words have to be designed!
When we were designing this book we tried . . .

curly, swirly letters

but they were too hard to read. We tried . . .

BIG, CHUNKY LETTERS

but we couldn't fit them all on the page. So we chose the style of letters you're reading now. **This style is a typeface called Avenir.**

Do you find it easy to read?

Do you think it looks good?

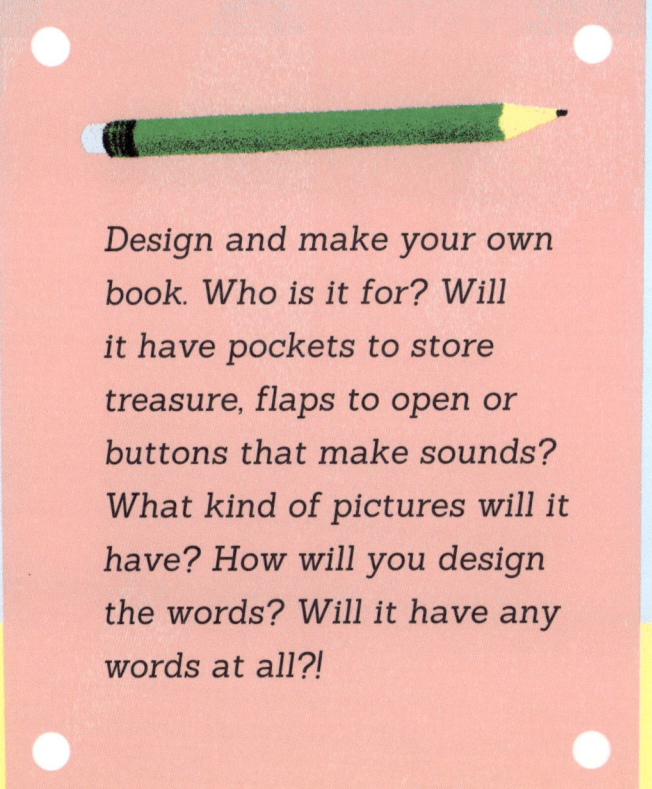

Design and make your own book. Who is it for? Will it have pockets to store treasure, flaps to open or buttons that make sounds? What kind of pictures will it have? How will you design the words? Will it have any words at all?!

The last thing you do each day is climb into bed . . . which one will you choose?

The Great Bed of Ware is the most famous bed in the world. It's more than three metres wide – big enough for eight people to sleep at once! It is even mentioned in one of Shakespeare's plays.

Sofa beds change from a sofa into a bed. They are good for small spaces. In this design, the arms slide down to complete the flat bed.

In Finland, every new baby is given a cardboard box which can be used as a simple bed!

This is the perfect place for a cat nap!

A bunk bed is a clever design: it makes the most of a smaller space. Some have desks or play areas underneath instead!

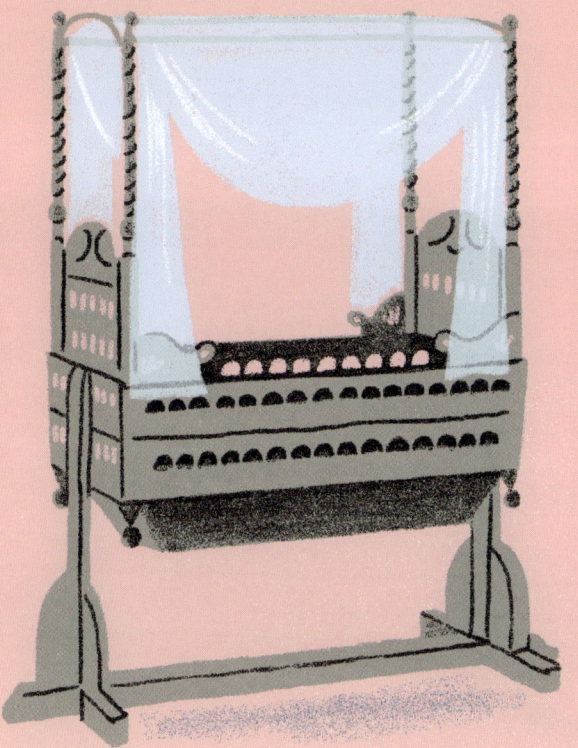

Daybeds have a very long seat, for napping or relaxing during the day.

Some beds are specially designed for children and babies. This cot was made in India. Nets hang from the frame to keep mosquitoes away.

How would you design your dream bed? Will it be long and wide for spreading out, or small to curl up in? Will you add comfy pillows and squishy cushions? Maybe there will be space underneath for all your favourite toys . . .

As you drift off to sleep, think about all the designs you came across in just one day. All of these things began in somebody's imagination.

An **imagination** just like yours!

Designs can be as small as a toothbrush . . .

or as **big** as a building!

Good design can make the ordinary
extraordinary.

All around the world, designers are hard at work solving problems.
They find out what people need. They try to make life better.
There are hundreds of different ways to be a designer.

Frank is an **architect**. He designs
lots of different buildings.

Monica is a **book designer**.
She designs all sorts of books.

Karl is a **fashion designer**. He designs
clothes, shoes and accessories.

Harriet is a **toy designer**.
She designs lots of toys.

What kind of designer would **you** like to be?

Samia is an **interior designer**.
She creates designs for inside rooms.

Rob is a **set designer**. He designs
scenery for the theatre, TV and films.

Jane is a **mechanical engineer**. She creates
designs for new technology, like rockets.

What will **you** design?

Credits

The Victoria and Albert Museum is the world's leading museum of art and design and houses over 2.3 million objects spanning over 5,000 years of humans creativity. Many illustrations in this book were inspired by items in the V&A collection – see if you can recognize them!

These items include:

Cover
'Bofinger' stacking chairs
Designed by Bätzner Architectural Office
with Rudolf Baresel-Bofinger, Karlsruhe,
1964–65, made by Menzolit-Werke,
Kraichtal-Menzingen, 1966
V&A: CIRC.435-1970

Pages 6–7
'Colorado' teapot
Designed by Marco Zanini, made by
Ceramiche Flavia, Italy, 1983
V&A: C.207 to A-1985

'Fresco Loft' high chair
Designed and made by Bloom,
Hong Kong, 2007
V&A: B.92-2010
Given by Bloom

Pages 8–9
'Bofinger' stacking chairs
Designed by Bätzner Architectural Office with
Rudolf Baresel-Bofinger, Karlsruhe, 1964–65
V&A: CIRC.435-1970

'Alfie Funghi' child's desk and stool
Designed by Philippe Starck for TOG, Italy,
2014–15
V&A: B.49-2015

'Fresco Loft' high chair
Designed and made by Bloom,
Hong Kong, 2007
V&A: B.92-2010
Given by Bloom

'HappyCat' beanbag chair
Designed by Christine Schwarzer and
Anne Birgitte Balle for Roommate,
Copenhagen, 2006
V&A: B.95-2010
Given by Roommate

Pages 10–11
Dress and headscarf
Designed by Diane Meyersohn, London, 1967
V&A: MISC.23&A-1988
Given by the designer

Dungarees
OshKosh B'Gosh Inc., USA, c. 1984
V&A: MISC.714-1992
Given by Kristina Byler Clark

Children's shoes
Made by C.S. Gilman, England, c. 1851
V&A: T.276&A-1963
Given by the maker

Moon shoes
England, 1950s–60s
V&A: B.3-2016
Given by Alan Craft

Crocs shoes
Crocs, Italy, 2007
V&A: B.188:1 to 5-2009

Pages 12–13
Children's shoes
Made by C.S. Gilman, England, about 1851
V&A: T.276&A-1963

Moon shoes
England, 1950s–60s
V&A: B.3-2016
Given by Alan Craft

Crocs
Crocs, Italy, 2007
V&A: B.188:1 to 5-2009

Pages 18–19
'Bofinger' stacking chairs
Designed by Bätzner Architectural Office with
Rudolf Baresel-Bofinger, Karlsruhe, 1964–65
V&A: CIRC.435-1970

Pages 24–25
'Spacehopper'
Great Britain, 1970s
V&A: B.18-2001
Given by Sandie Cox

Pages 26–27
Silk umbrella
England, 1840-50
V&A: T.77-1923

Umbrella with vulture handle
Great Britain, 1900-29
V&A: T.222-1995

'Storm' red umbrella
Designed by Senz°, Delft, 2004-05
V&A: T.2:1, 2-2015

Pages 28–29

'Super Helta Skelta' gravity toy
Kiddicraft Ltd Hestair, England, 1984
V&A: MISC.191-1989
Given by the manufacturer

'Qubis Haus' dolls' house
Designed and made by Amy Whitworth,
United Kingdom, 2014
V&A: B.95:1 to 8-2014

Constructional set
Lott's Bricks Ltd, Watford, 1918–20
V&A: B.32:1 to 5-2004
Given by Raymond Foster

Toy helicopter
South Africa, 1990–94
V&A: B.94-1995
Given by Nelson Mandela and Janey Buchan

Pages 30–31

Toy helicopter
South Africa, 1990–94
V&A: B.94-1995
Given by Nelson Mandela and Janey Buchan

Pages 32–33

Bird bath toy
Designed by Patrick Rylands
for Trendon Ltd, England, 1970
V&A: MISC.41-1970
Given by Trendon Ltd

Fish bath toy
Designed by Patrick Rylands
for Trendon Ltd, England, 1970
V&A: MISC.42-1970
Given by Trendon Ltd

'Clyde' cabin cruiser
Lines Bros. Ltd, England, about 1969
V&A: B.262:1, 2-2010
Given by Roger Gilham

Pages 34–35

'Bookworm' bookshelf
Designed by Ron Arad, London, 1993,
made by Kartell, Milan, 1995
V&A: W.2-1996

'Alfie Funghi' child's desk and stool
Designed by Philippe Starck for TOG, Italy,
2014–15
V&A: B.49-2015

'Bibibibi' lamp with legs
Designed by Ingo Maurer,
Munich, 1982
M.23-1992

'Hebi' table lamp
Designed by Isao Hosoe
for Valenti & Co., Milan, 1971
V&A: CIRC.507-1973

Elephant chair
Designed by Charles and Ray Eames,
1945, made by Vitra, Switzerland, 2007
V&A: B.257-2009

Artichoke lamp
Designed by Poul Henningsen
for Louis Poulsen, Copenhagen, 1960
V&A: M.38-1992

'Atollo 233' table lamp
Designed by Vico Magistretti
for Oluce, Milan, 1977
V&A: M.39-1992
Given by the Property Services Agency (PSA),
a division of the Department of the Enviroment.

Pages 36–37

'Bookworm' bookshelf
Designed by Ron Arad, London, 1993,
made by Kartell, Milan, 1995
V&A: W.2-1996

Pages 38–39

Great Bed of Ware
Made by Hans Vredeman de Vries,
Probably Ware, 1590–1600
V&A: W47:1 to 28-1931
Purchased with Art Fund support

'JI1' sofa bed
Designed by James Irvine, Milan, 1992,
made by CBI, Stockholm, 1997
V&A: W.15-1997

Day bed
Made by Jean-Baptiste Tilliard I, Paris,
about 1750
V&A: W.5:1, 2-1956
Bequeathed by Edith Beatty to Sir Alfred
Chester Beatty, by whom given to the
Museum in her memory

Cradle
Unknown, Coromandel Coast, 1660–80
V&A: IS.15-1983

Pages 40–41

'Bibibibi' lamp with legs
Designed by Ingo Maurer,
Munich, 1982
M.23-1992

Pages 45–46

'Spacehopper'
Great Britain, 1970s
V&A: B.18-2001
Given by Sandie Cox

PUFFIN BOOKS

UK | USA | Canada | Ireland | Australia | India | New Zealand | South Africa

Puffin Books is part of the Penguin Random House group of companies
whose addresses can be found at global.penguinrandomhouse.com.

www.penguin.co.uk   www.puffin.co.uk   www.ladybird.co.uk

First published 2020
001

Printed in China
A CIP catalogue record for this book is available from the British Library

ISBN: 978–0–241–38013–0

All correspondence to: Puffin Books, Penguin Random House Children's
One Embassy Gardens, New Union Square
5 Nine Elms Lane, London SW8 5DA